POEMS NOT MEANT TO BE READ: A Journey of Self-Discovery
By: Zosha Durano

First Edition
United States of America

ISBN: 979-8-218-87394-3
Cover art by Zosha Durano
Interior design by Zosha Durano

Author's Note

This is a story of coming out, depression, self-harm, suicidality, eating disorders, biraciality, and within all of that hope, healing, belonging, and love. Pain didn't strengthen me. The love around me and within me gave me courage to find the strength I needed. Which took an epic journey to discover I already had. I always did. Love is around and within you even if it feels more like a fleck of ash than a brick of stone. Our hearts pulsate with bravery more than it does blood.

Dedicated to all those who accidentally saved my life–most of you know who you are and those who you don't, know that I wouldn't be here without you. Thank you. I love you.

Table of Contents:

Part I: DEPRESSION'S DIARY

1. The Side Character

Proclaim me as the side character
The one living in the blank margins of the protagonist's forever
unfurling scroll
Only slipping into the patterned pools of ink for a chapter, a page, or a
paragraph
My birth, life, and death happen someplace behind the coverings of
the book
So small and quiet it fits snugly in a single fiber of the binding
The text tells me I am a thousand-piece puzzle with several pieces
missing and likely never to be found
A thousand orbiting solar systems
Stirring inside an existence so quiet it won't be heard above a hushed
whisper

2. Tally Marks

They say they don't understand the tally marks on my body
I tell them is a scoreboard
It is keeping record of the ups and downs of this beautiful yet vicious
game
The one in which you are betting against yourself
It's surviving the bombing trenches in the middle of a battlefield
And in its quiet aftermath picking up the remaining shrapnel as
souvenirs to hang around your neck
It is running from a forest fire
With smoke and flame turning into monster jaws to swallow you
whole
And finding that the place where the racing pulse steadies
Is the heart in which the fire burns the hardest
It's knowing you deserve the Cross
So you crucify yourself with the cheap rusted nails you have on hand
To have proof to present to the mirror
That you are paying for your sins
It is both the hurricane and the debris
Both the compass and the cliff
Both Peter's sword and Jesus' thorned crown
They say they still don't understand
I tell them I don't either

3. Tally Marks, part 2

They ask me, what are you keeping track of that is so dire the writing belongs nowhere else but your flesh?
It is a countdown
Microdosing death
It is an album
Memories branded forever
It is a log
Debts still being paid
It is a quota
How much closer am I?

4. Tally Marks, part 3

Long sleeves at the beach
Sweaters in the sun
Pants in the water
How many quirks can you tally before it starts to sting?

5. Poems Not Meant to be Read

Poems not meant to be read
Words not meant to be said
Speak them when I am dead
Buried alive instead
In storms I make my bed
Anthems bleed in my head
While text fills the page like lead

6. A Self-Portrait of Dysthymia

The brush strokes of this painting are not a thousand poisoned blades
sawing through the canvas in fast-motion
They are just a soft drizzle that slowly rusts its fibers with each gentle
tap

The colors are not a hurricane of emotions exploding out of the
picture one after the other nonstop to replace words and air with tears
and screams
They are just a swirl of loneliness subtly shaded into a single dark
cloud on a day of sunshine and blue skies

The frame is not a metal shackle chaining the body to its bed to
immobilize all movement in its mind and limbs
It's just a blanket of fatigue that does not let energy exceed
half-capacity except in rare bursts that drain it for the rest of the day

The easel is not standing on the edge of the cliff with only the heels of
its feet grazing the platform and the rest of it already meeting the
other side of emptiness
It's just thinking of its weight and once in a while idealizing an artist
that would have simply allowed it to remain vacant

The shading is not a piercing blackness that swallows every inch of
vibrancy into its hungry belly
It's just an underlying grey that comes and goes so quietly and
politely its footsteps are hardly heard

This painting crumbles into pebbles and not boulders
But pebbles still cause ripples in the water
And those ripples are echoing in every end of this moonless sea
Every so often collecting into an unforgiving tsunami
That will ravage all in its path
Its colors bleeding shadow into the earth

7. A Failed Coming-Out

I grew up collecting shards of glass casually tossed to the ground
They cut my hands but they were no bigger than paper cuts
Today I decided to compile them into a stained glass window
Painting over the sharp edges with excuses and reasons and dismissals
Making them unite as something other than a large blade
Turning them into what I wanted them to be
Even if the pieces made it clear they did not fit right
And would not fit in the way I was trying to force them to
And now I spend the nighttime thinking
Thinking of the role I wish I continued to play, the one that made you applaud every time
The sound of approval filling up the hungry auditorium of my soul
While my body ached and withered behind the curtain
Was it foolishness or hope?

8. How?

Part of me wishes you didn't mean as much to me as you did
Because then each smile wouldn't make my heart ache
Each melodic note wouldn't turn into melancholic drizzle
Each flap of wings wouldn't give me whiplash

Part of me wishes I didn't mean as much to me as I did
Because then I could go back to when my soul was an ant and my
body was a boot
The vessel constantly betraying its trusting and naive passenger
Invalidation and fear squishing it until it became one with the empty
void of forgotten thoughts and lost dreams

But I have let it breathe
The first gasp of air after a lifetime of being buried alive without even
knowing it, the compact dirt having become oxygen, rejuvenated like
nothing else
And now my soul knows life instead of entrapment
And it can't be buried again

Yet for you I find myself searching for the shovel
For you
I find myself grappling for the script that I can read off of to say the
words you want to hear
The ones that will make your soul flutter

Because what I want is for both of us to fly together
The wind flapping in our faces and rushing through our hair
Our vast galaxies merging into one set of mesmerizing constellations
that do not need to be compromised or softened
That can be observed for the beauty they behold in all that they
currently are and have always been

How can something be so liberating and so suffocating at the same time?

9. The Perfect Me

I am strong
Stomach flat but sculpted with abs, little grooves on a mountain that
can't be moved and can't be overcome
Muscles toned all the way through
I flex them in the mirror just for fun, the glass sweating as it realizes
what a fortunate viewer it is
My skin-tight dresses smile as they press warmly against my body
and merge into my meadowy skin that's soft with the grasses that
blow in the wind but firm enough to carry the world on its solid soil
I run the fastest and lift the most of everyone in the gym
No one's head turns as I lift the maximum weight like it's Mjolnir and
I'm the only one worthy
Because they've all come to get used to the crackles of lightning
between my fingers
Perspiration only dribbles down my forehead, natural beads of
jewelry that serve as polite reminders of my mortality
And they smell of Bora Bora waters or nothing at all
My pants are a steady rhythm that doesn't follow a metronome but
sets its own that everyone else scrambles to follow
I am perfectly strong

10. The Perfect Me, part 2

I am beautiful
My skin is a clear landscape that gleams from each end of the
horizon,
The light of the day reflecting off it and making it sparkle brighter
than constellations on a dark night in the country
My face is a blossoming flower
My lips its perfect petals
Surrounding a collection of world-class pearls that cause onlookers to
faint at their glory
My eyes are not a pool of brown
But an abyss of coffee so rich it could cure world hunger twice and so
delicate it could shatter with a single touch
Sprinkles of honey freckled within and revealed in the glint of the sun
Bordered by impeccably long eyelashes that curve right where they
need to, each one distinct and full of its own life
My hair is long and flowing
The wind can't help but beg it to be its playmate just so it can run its
fingers through each smooth and luscious fiber
Never able to tangle it no matter how fascinated it gets because
nothing can ever ruin it
It always falls perfectly in place
Not like law-abiding soldiers who base their lives on rigor but like a
sea of carefree dreamers that dance freely yet never miss a step
I am perfectly beautiful

11. The Perfect Me, part 3

I am likable
The lights of a room exceed their brightest setting the moment I step foot in it
I open my mouth and nothing but music comes pouring out, without spending a single minute glancing at the songbook beforehand
I live in the perfect interval between confident and humble
Striding into business meetings instead of job interviews, the CEO handing over their position before I even finish introducing myself out of enchantment at the sound of my voice
But still the type of person strangers who have lived decades of solidarity strip their souls in front of since my smile is just that inviting and true
My advice is like a healer's hands, washing away every pain and dilemma and leaving nothing but joy and wholeness
In every conversation I braid comedy, sentimentality, and seriousness into one perfect French braid
For my demeanor is as comfortable and my voice is as clear and my thoughts are as quick with a friend, a crush, a peer, and a superior as they are with myself
I don't have a mask and I don't fumble to do magic tricks
Because the magic everyone admires and applauds is in the transparent window of my soul
I am perfectly likable

12. The Perfect Me, part 4

I am smart
I read a cluster of foreign words once and it is forever ingrained in my brain like an exotic tattoo I am proud of I am so inked up I give rappers a run for their money
Little-known but always-relevant trivia can't help but spurt out of me like water out of the fringes of an overloaded cup
People gather around to listen to me lecture about all the topics they care about
I am never afraid to express a controversial opinion
Or play the devil's advocate in a room full of angels because I know by the time I finish my sentence everyone will have traded their wings for horns
I bound around a room containing a million booby traps with my eyes closed,
My feet always knowing right where to land before my brain sends it a detailed fax because my mind and body are always a single unit of grace and dignity
My hands never shake
My eyes never miss a detail
I never make a mistake
My winning streak is as long as the days I've been alive
My accomplishments are as long as the Guinness book of world records, because my talents are headlining every page and I know it
This is the perfect me

13. Bi

Bisexual
Biracial
But what I'm learning is two halves do not make a whole
They jut out and poke sharply
Not pearly enough to be the moon
Not radiant enough to be the sun
Instead trying to burrow a nest in the night sky
But the black landscape is desolate and lonely
Reaching out to both sides
But where is a hand to hold?

14. Hunger

Here I am in front of my mirror
Underlining the overspilling excesses
Negating the contradicting hollowness within
Go a little longer, dig a little deeper
Eject that poison though my soul begs it to stay
Reject my reflection though the cracks are manmade

15. Teach Me

Teach me to be strong
Teach me to be confident and radiate self-belief
Teach me to have eyes that burn straight into those that dare challenge me
Teach me to have feet anchored to the ground to keep my back tall and chin up
Teach me to have skin like armor

Not metal pierced and cracked by the arrows of ridicule and self-doubt
Not feet wavering and unsteady and drifting into obscurity from the smallest winter breeze
Not a spine with prickly ticks that make it so I'm only comfortable when my back is slouched

Teach me to be strong
Teach me to keep my aim from quivering like a tremor and my target from shifting every time I blink
Teach me to hear my own voice in this crowded room

16. 3 am

It's 3 am and I can't sleep
Thoughts are racing through my mind
So fast they outrun my ability to comprehend them
They're just blurs that flash across
Too quick for me to flag down
Yet slow enough for me to see in their entirety
So that I know that the smiles and winks they send me are not
courteous and kind but snide and taunting
They crash into one another and jostle my brain with the chaos they
create

It's 3 am and every longing is digging its way into my heart
My chest is as hard as concrete
But each random and not-so-random thought and feeling has its own
shovel that effortlessly pierces through
And they make themselves home until I am filled with emptiness—
Something that isn't supposed to take up space yet is overflowing
within me
And I ache with loneliness and melancholy
For no particular reason at all

It's 3 am and I am wide awake
Forget the fatigue of my body
Forget the boredom
My brain refuses to acknowledge them
In a few hours I'll hear the birds chirping
It will piss the hell out of me
Before I feel guilty for being so angry at how happy they sound

It's 3 am and I can't sleep

17. Make Sure You're Heard

"Make sure you're heard"
Sounds like a casual yet kind comment
Advice given in passing
But I can't describe how those four words are so profound to me
How they make me think and wonder -
How many times have I silenced my own voice to let others speak?
How many times have I ripped the vocal chords out of my own throat
to amplify someone else's?
How many times have I let others trample over me so they could be
elevated?
How many times have I clawed at my own mind and body and soul
for the sole purpose of clawing at them until they bled and withered
and shrunk?
Over and over and over again
I don't even realize I'm doing it anymore
My shriveled soul cries to me, "You owe me"
"I've endured your kicks after your repeated stabbings"
"I've gasped for breath through shattered lungs just to make myself
keep breathing after you deflated me of life"
"I'm tired of my pulsating heartbeat being drowned out by the
splitting taunts that have become the background noise to my life"
"I deserve better than your continual abuse and the continual abuse
you stood by and watched me take"
"But I stick around because you need me"
"I stick around because one day you'll let me speak and you'll be
astounded at the music I can make"
"Why can't you fight for me?"
"Why can't you let me be heard?"
"I deserve that"
"You owe me that"

18. Words From Whispering Voices

I hold the metal above the barrier between my soul and this world
Until a soft wind kisses my bruised knuckles
And a fleck of light tickles my torn cheeks

Their voices come in whispers
"My dear"
"One day life will taste as sweet as candy instead of that dry ache that
stings your throat"
"One day humor will rumble your landscape instead of that
earthquake that perforates your lungs"

"I don't want to wait" I tell them

They smile at me
"My dear today"
"Today you have a candle that chases every shadow in the room"
"Today you have a song that makes a whole room glow"
"Let me light it so you can feel its incandescence"
"Let me amplify it so you can hear what we do"

Part II: THE ANONYMOUS AUTOBIOGRAPHY

19. The Runners

Some days I feel I must be a monster
A chemical flask knocked over by a great scientist's astute elbow
His first error in a lifetime of trials
Crafting a product that hisses in sunlight and burns to the touch

But you
You run to me when you see me
You with your pawpads that slip on floorboards not made for you
You with your miniature feet so newly crafted the mold has barely
dried
You with your aged footsteps that tiptoe in sunlight to beware of
shadows
You with your heavy shackles that drag a shipload of fatigue and pain

But you run to me when you see me
Your eyes light up with electricity
Your mouth opens into a gaping hole
Not a scream
But a beaming smile

I can't be a monster then
Or I am and still you love me

20. Thank You For Teaching Me Self-Love

You named my eyes starlight and moonlight
And now I feel explosions of sun between my lashes every time I blink

You caressed my hair way wind brushes a sunflower field
And now I feel the glow of each strand like a dose of rainbow shimmer

You danced to the motion of the tremors disrupting my hands' firm grasp
And now I feel electricity between my fingertips as I stretch them to stroke the clouds

You picked out the accent in my voice like it was a seashell among miles of golden ground
And now I feel a microphone placed neatly beneath my throat with each proud word

You drank my laughter as if it was water from the purest of springs
And now I feel a halo around my head from the light rays that beam off of it when I toss it backwards

You framed my palms as I swiped them over touch-deprived souls caked in dust
And now I feel a mirror on my knuckles reflecting back to my skin the love I give to the world

21. Gold

The rain pours hard
The thunder cries loudly
The lightning strikes ferociously
But each of us is a fractal of shining light
A gem of color that twinkles night and day
We are both the colorful bridge
And the gold at the end of it

22. Why?

Why should I chip away at my soul to make it easier for you to grasp?
The edges are pointy like the ends of a star
Not like the knife you make it out to be
You don't have to shield your palms

Its incandescence is like the heart of a sun
With a warmth that when nurtured can be strong enough to hold the
world in a tender embrace
Not like the conflagration that you believe it to be
You don't have to avert your eyes

Its heartbeat is like a butterfly's fluttering wings
A simple liberating beauty that gently takes you to new heights
Not like the thumping battle drums that you think you hear
You don't have to muffle your ears

Why should I negotiate who I am into a compromise between the
great galaxy that my soul holds and the tiny cracked lens you choose
to view it out of?

23. Two

1+1 does not always equal 2
Not when 1 is a striped cloth that sings out constellations
Not when 1 is a blue and red that bursts with sun and stars
They bleed together
They make a new color
A new sky
A new number
They hold text that needs its own transcription
Language that needs its own tongue
Culture that needs its own party
For there is twice as much to celebrate

24. What I Mean When I Say You're My Favorite

I've memorized the notes of your laughter
It is my favorite song

I've memorized the scene frames of your eyebrows
It is my favorite movie

I've memorized the silhouette of your bones
It is my favorite dance

I've memorized the fall of your hair
It is my favorite landscape

I've memorized the waves of your voice
It is my favorite ocean

I've memorized the speckles of your eyes
It is my favorite constellation

I'm memorizing the rhythm of your heartbeat
It will be my map back home

25. I Guess Not

I thought I was made of solid brick
Not a single peephole to expose the thousands of gears creaking and
rusting against each other
Not a single crack to permit air to shudder the fragile skeleton a whiff
away from disintegration
Not a single pocket to enter light upon the unending rows of withering
crops left only for the starved rats

But you take one look at me and turn me into glass

Except through this transparent pane
My gears sing melodies and shine with gold as they rub together
Oxygen caresses a fleshed body that dances to the echoes of its own
sorrowful yet prideful anthem
Starlight bursts over fields of budding flowers that flocks of birds
perch upon as respite from a long journey

Suddenly I don't mind being made of glass

26. Recover

Reflection, I stand here, no longer waiting for the crack
Enemies are what I made out of the blood in my veins
Capillaries are not made to be gnashed open
Organs are not made to be vacuumed clean
Victory is mine every time my teeth find a home in food
Excess is beauty, beauty is strength
Rippling my soul with the replenishment of my bones

27. Dressing Up

These feet are the feet that have walked me across miles of glass shards
Let me slip them into dazzling heels that click proudly with each step

These hands are the hands that have held together my lungs and intestines as they tore out of my skin
Let me adorn them with bracelets that twinkle like stars

These fingers are the fingers that have written out my name in blood when the rest of me could not move
Let me decorate them with nails that serve as pocket sized rainbows

This stomach is the stomach that has absorbed punches from knuckle brasses that reverberated through my entire being
Let me fill it with delicacies that are the world's greatest delights and the guiltiest of pleasures

These eyes are the eyes that led me through valleys filled with vines that turned into snakes
Let me paint them with colors and lines that dazzle into vibrancy that cannot be muted

This body is the body that has stayed my truest ally in all that I've been and haven't been
Let me serenade it with a song that lulls it to peace from its wars

28. The Mirror

Not shuddering at the lines of my reflection
Instead tracing them so they transform into frames of my
constellations
Not letting them fade me into obscurity
Instead emboldening them so they highlight my presence
Not shrinking them into nothing until I disappear with them
Instead magnifying them so they make me take up the entire room
Let's not be afraid to exist
In all that we are

29. Learning to Live

My aim still quivers and the target still shifts with each release
But my arrows land on the board now instead of littering the ground
My legs still limp and my knees still wobble like a newborn fawn
with each step
But my feet march forward now instead of dragging backwards
My voice still trembles and the room still is overstuffed with noisy
crowds
But my words are louder now than they've ever been

30. More

The whispering voices come back
But they are louder now
Not a shout
But a steady declaration in sentences that for once end in periods and
not question marks

"My dear," they state
"You are more than your worst mistakes
"You are brighter than the darkness that tries every day to swallow
you
"You are more than a word or even a sentence
"Even if the distance between the capital letter and the period is
farther than the opposite ends of the world, it would never be big
enough to fill everything that you are
"You are too much to comprehend"

"Your soul is vast, not empty
"Your glass is chipped, not shattered
"The rust of your existence is a sign of your mortality but does not
mean you are dying"

"Stop tearing chunks of yourself to squeeze into boxes that simplify
you
"Stop simplifying yourself
"You are not simple
"You are confusing and contradicting
"Your paint strokes are big and bold and crazed
"You are more than anyone will ever know
"You are more than you will ever admit
"You are more"

31. Broken Society

We live in a broken society
A shattered mirror of a world with so many cracks we cannot see our
own reflections
We pour everything inside us trying to pick up these shards of glass
But all we end up with are cut hands
Blood tainting what we once and tried once more to hold close
But our souls glow on
They flicker, only a small candlelight flame amid a million tornadoes
bulldozing through the earth for no reason except to stir up the dirt
where our feet are planted
They wane until they're only a speck of light in the black tapestry of
the night sky
You have to squint in order to see your own ember
Pat your hands around the air like a blind man without a walking stick
to find the other flames
But when your fingers crash against the orange warmth the coldness
soothes
The cuts sting a little less intensely
And you realize we are not tiny dots in a dark world
We are the stars
Bold and beautiful and breathing
Twinkling so hard it's like they're dancing
And we don't need a mirror to peer into ourselves or into one another
Interlock your fingers with mine
Let some of the blood you haven't stopped bleeding since the cruel
hand of life struck you seep into me
And I will carry it in my veins and let my heart pump your story into
my soul
My flesh is but a thin covering of the rickety bones that make up my
body, perforated by permanent wounds that still throb every time they
are poked

But light leaks into them every time you touch my soul, accidentally
or purposely
And I hope you feel this same respite every time I look at you
We cannot save the world
We cannot fix each other
Sometimes we cannot even help ourselves
But we can lay together in the rubble of humanity
We can find fairy tales in the storm clouds that swirl above us
We can let the shadows outline the beauty that is our existence

32. The Anonymous Autobiography

Still don't know who this writer is
Still don't know what this story is about
Or where it's headed
But I'll sit with the text on the pages
I'll let the chapters scroll on

33. The Flawed Protagonist

I don't make for a clean story with a linear plot line,
To be praised by the highest of critics for its relevant lessons and
remarkable themes
I would be riddled with so many plot holes my life would be confused
with a neglected road
I would make the reader raise their eyebrows so much their forehead
aches, and suspend their disbelief so much they forget the definition
of logic
My decisions and traits would swish so rapidly back and forth they'd
cause whiplash
There is no simple, clear lesson to be learned
No definitive trait to model one's self after
Just a character and a story
Just a human and a life
Too bright to stare at directly for very long
Like the sparkling stars that light up the dark sky as if they're
precious diamonds in a cave
The moon in a solar eclipse that trips in front of something so much
bigger and more powerful than itself
Something it can never understand and never touch
I am too confusing and conflicting to shine a light on for longer than a
minute
Too imperfect to understand
Too big to hold between two hands
A thousand-piece puzzle with several pieces missing and likely never
to be found
A thousand orbiting solar systems
Bursting beyond the text now in cheers that tear the pages
I am flawed but I am alive
I am flawed but this story is mine now

www.ingramcontent.com/pod-product-compliance
Lightning Source LLC
Chambersburg PA
CBHW070453130626
46553CB00006B/2393